Imprint

To each, *her* own

Natasha Pai Sansguiri

INDIA • SINGAPORE • MALAYSIA

To the little version of us, looking for more.

Contents

Foreword

Natasha Pai Sansguiri is a mercurial talent possessed of such a wide range of skills and interests that it comes as no surprise that she is an Arian. Aries are said to be natural leaders, pioneers and go-getters who are ambitious and passionate about their work. They are known for their drive, competitiveness, and determination to succeed.. all characteristics which personify this young bundle of beauty and brains.

I first connected with Natasha when she did her first book, *Fathers Are Forever*, which instantly went on to become a bestseller. It was a daughter's tribute to the memory of her father, and as such, a heartfelt and touching account of their life together that reached out to every daughter who has shared an extraordinary bond with her own father. My interactions with Natasha during the production and publication of this book, forged a friendship of shared joys and grief, mutual understanding and respect.

On a professional level, Natasha is a Corporate Legal counsel based out of Bengaluru, having done her Masters in Business law at the National Law School there. Academically, she has been a topper in Goa, She is a hands-on mother to her daughter, Alia and her four pets, leading a wholesome life nurturing, reading, staying fit, and pursuing a career that keeps her mentally engaged at every stage of her momentous, admirable life.

Having so many passions and having excelled in so many areas of endeavours, I wasn't really taken aback to learn that this lively and deceptively diminutive powerhouse is also a poet. I shall leave it to the established poets and that bane of writers everywhere, the critics, to comment on Natasha's poetry in terms of style and technique. I will only say this, that as a reader, *Imprint,* most adequately meets my own criteria for good writing..... it is honest and unpretentious, and more importantly, it has *soul.*

– Sapna Sardessai
February 26, 2025

[Sapna Sardessai is a Publisher, Restaurateur and former Journalist, based in Goa. Established in 2003, her Advertising and Publishing firm Printer's Devil has produced over 150 notable publications. She runs two restaurants in Candolim and Panjim called Kokum Curry that showcase traditional Goan Saraswat cuisine.]

Preface

Poems are not written in ink but in the pauses, glances, chances and silence between two people.

Acknowledgment

Quite strangely, I am thankful for what we call the midlife adversities one has to encounter that offer to take you through the journey and teach you lessons in many ways. By this time, the roses go away, and we rise to ourselves. We experience loss in the form of the death of a loved one, a career crashing down or turning a different way, and a child teaching you kindness in new ways. A phase that gives you new reasons to try again after a nasty fall, people walk out to create a space for those who are meant to walk in and stay for long, providing a real break-free to begin a ride called alignment.

Disconnected

We choose one another the second time,
With a hope to see a different side.

To endure a routine of our own,
not together yet peacefully alone,
we look at the past on the outside,
we heal the wounds and bid them goodbye.

Perspective is all that changed,
to get what you want and so do I,
we settle for different things,
after choosing a different side.

Doormat

As invisible as air, I stand here,
waiting for a brief conversation,
longing to connect since past few years,
forgetting that you came only to leave an ordeal.

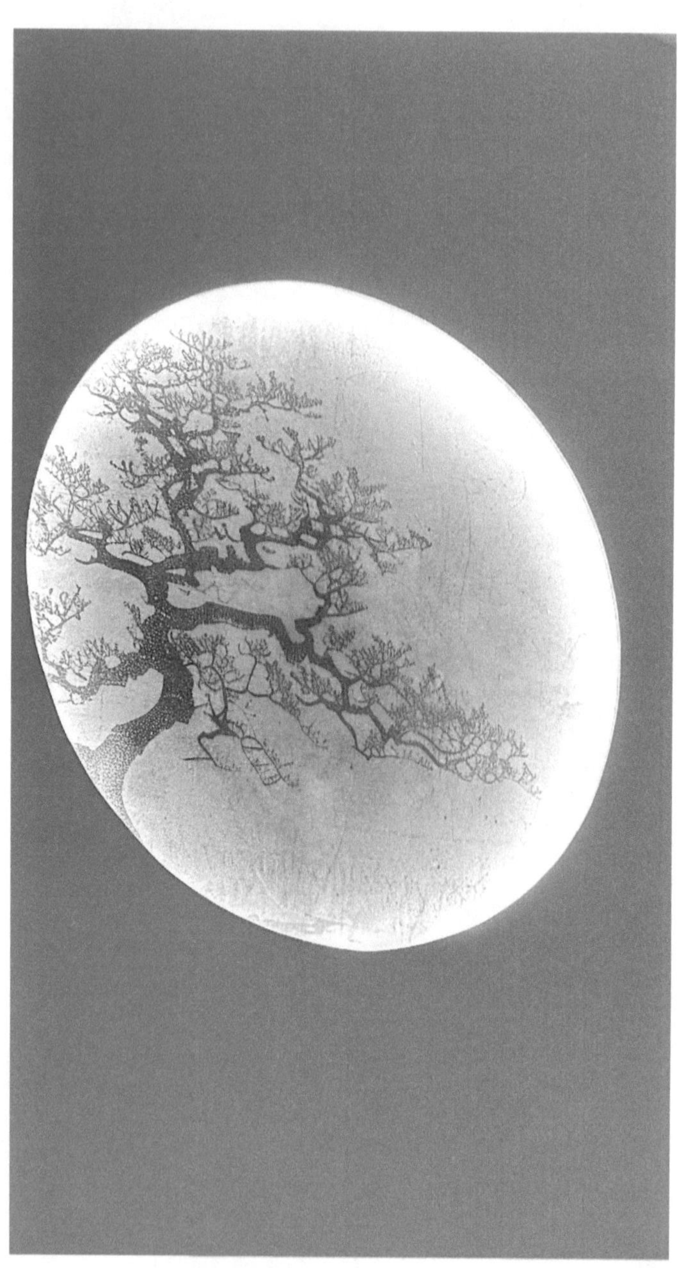

Unknown

Thinking of the future, building clouds of worry,
what is yet to come, I wish I could foresee.

Thinking of the past, memories hold me its prisoner,
wondering how could I ever let all that happen.

Living in the now, I see what nature has to offer,
leaves fall, still the tree stands tall,
embracing the unknown every season,
unveiling a new chapter for a reason!

Adventure
is Out there

Milestone

Unless you are willing to disrupt everything that is,
you shall see no end.

Grieve as it pains, in circles or waves,
let silence break you and art blend again.

Rising from the ashes of failure too is a milestone,
that changes the game.

Offspring

Offspring asked me one day if I was her friend or
mother?
I felt its nice to be friends, but still, I will choose to be
the latter.

Hearing my answer, disappointment showed up at
instantly.
Let her wonder I said, while remaining curious for
further questioning.

To remain important or worthy was no longer the bone
of contention,
we both are opinionated and ready for a dimension.

Desiring to see her independent, I would rather first
be present,
being tired or done is not our way, let us understand
how to begin.

Keeping it light and always bright is not my intention,
leading her into a niche of her own, is the purpose of
procreation.

The end is all that matters we hear often,
you are not my crutch for an old age, and I will love
you through my struggles.

Understand that the path you choose and the pain
you endure will be felt by me too,
but I will not pull you back and fight your battles.

At times when you fear, I'll hold your hand and whisper,
if you need me ever, you will have your *Mother*!

Choice

Heart that is dissatisfied, pitied and rigged,
gamble is the new name to reach.
Uncertainty is the bean so magical,
patience is the only virtue indeed.

Heart that is made up of scars,
soul that lives by the shore,
there is a house glued with memories,
there is a goal to have it all.

Heart that is eager to know,
how, why, and when, what is destined to happen,
What is meant to be is already written,
Now we turn the page or close the book, is the question.

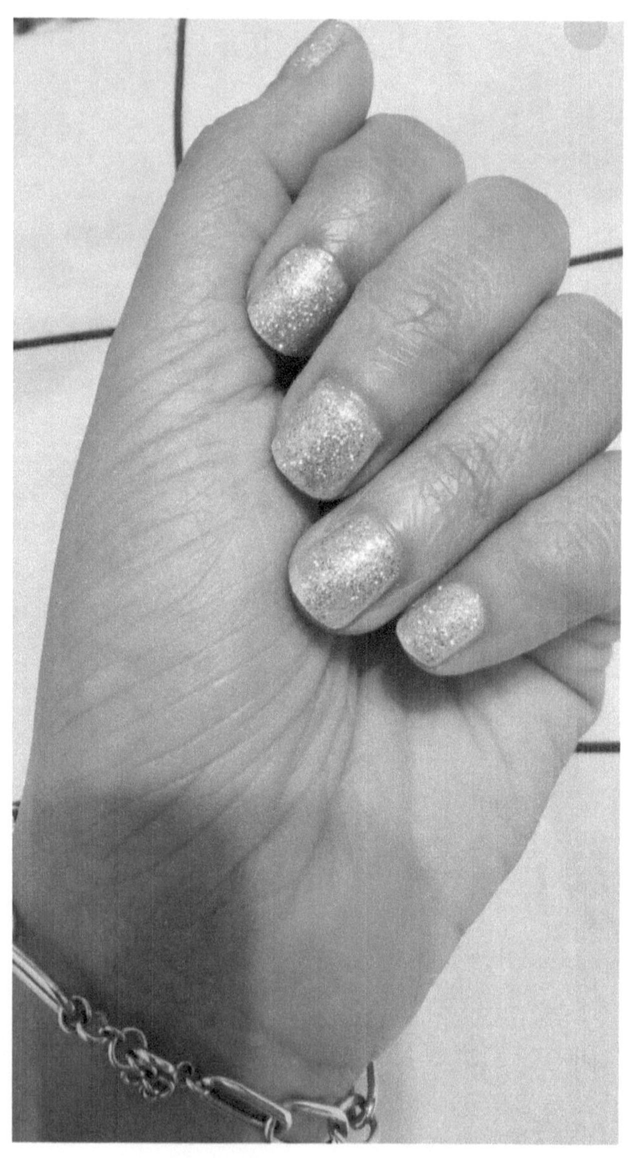

Bling

Loving a wrong person with your heart in the right place,
wishing for a peaceful association while it bleeds.

It is hard to stay, hard to walk away,
messy to clean up after it fails.

You wear your badges on the sleeves,
daughter, wife and mother it seems,
holding on to this delusion feels necessary,
bling is the theme, you dress up accordingly.

Home

Warm hugs and blankets, so rare,
someone still checking if you have been fed,
no agenda and expectations attached,
you are here now, it is all that matters.

Little defeat or big crash,
come straight and fall in the lap,
collecting hope as we share,
only to hear, 'to rest first, and you'll get there'.

Smell of the old books still lingers,
decluttering gets us ready to figure,
blurry pictures and honours build the wall,
that is meant to be pulled down only when they are
gone.

Memories of a meal shared after being unfair,
water still being warmed up inspite of a despair,
leaving for a dream house with stairs,
Home is still the person who's back there.

Memories

An empty list, something small to wish,
mundane days and errands to complete,
but I get a call to check if I live, at least.

Looking forward as the day ends,
friends gather, collecting moments,
raising a toast and appraising their story,
that I listened to, carefully.

Each day repeats miraculously,
days to memories instantly,
happy and alive in every story,
while achieving nothing extraordinary.

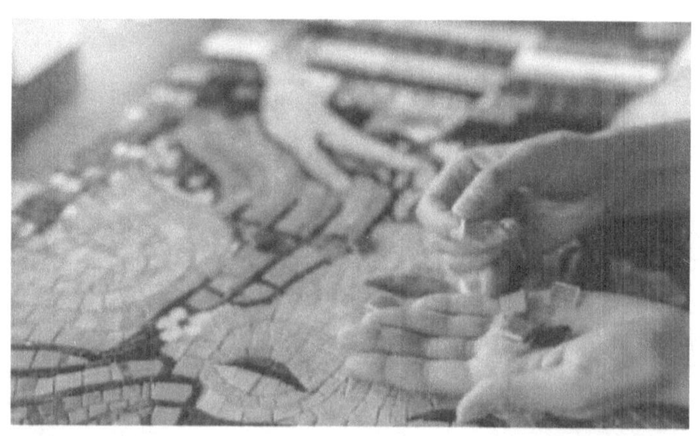

End

Chaos feels like it is winning,
yet collapse is the beginning,
we see the end when things fall apart,
but broken edges fit together becoming a mosaic,
falling into a design which doesn't seem like it now, as
right.

Unbound

Marriage, is not a union, or an institution,
neither a legally binding merger or an acquisition.

Heap of expectations build up to remain happy and
content,
companionship is mere convenience, while we partner
with intent.

You are complete, and so am I, you are exploring and
so do I,
rest when you should, says a voice that cares,
you are not my catalyst to grow, that's a lot to bear.

Tick tock goes the clock, time runs out as we count,
Yet we arrive when it is our turn, finding joy, just as
we are unbound!

Exist

The future of the rose blooming,
what was its form before, we think,
whether a kid will pluck it, or given as an offering,
whether the birds will destroy it or the wind may
sling.

Even when nothing out of the ordinary happens,
the rose still rises, blooms out of the bud,
blossoms and disappears into the earth,
living like a present, seizing the time,
talking with the wind, soaking in the sun,
fading away in the moonlight, just in time.

Unafraid to live in spite of the challenges,
surrounded by death for the few hours it *Exist*.

Version

Whenever I held myself back, you let me flow,
composing something new and raw.

Life without you has humbled me and hardened me at
the same time,
It has unmasked me and released me at the right time.

No success feels like whole without you taking pride
in it,
brings me to a very start, comforted by a brokenness
within.

Adversities I just walk in through are the vices,
because the pain feels like you, and the happiness too,
the journey feels like you and the destination too,
Because a little version of me, is still looking for you!

Evolve

First love, doesn't mean best love,
best friends, doesn't mean forever.

Crossing over a phase that existed for a brief,
memories collected and innocence we killed.

Knowing someone, somewhere, did care once,
sending love to our versions that dared evolution.

Grief

Losing a loved one, takes you back in time,
an eerie silence, a song, an old t-shirt worn out,
with illusion to mend that's fallen apart.

Memories of the time we wish to have heard you often,
did just as you said, without any hesitation.

Smiling through the dream, we wake up breaking down,
trying to hold you a little closer during the visiting hour...

It's hard to relate to how far we've moved along,
more forgiving and accepting of unexpressed love,
letting go and grieving until you loosen whats hardened,
Grief is a time we wished to have travelled backward.

Affair

The perfect time after imbalance,
sequel that completes unfinished,
holding space to fall again,
this time for yourself, a messy *Affair*.

Alignment

A wave takes us in, while we struggle,
enough of these swings, we mutter,
a voice in our head finds a thread,
we hold on tightly planning a decamp.

Moments of adversity test our character,
we take it in, or avoid it as pleasant,
cycles repeat, looping in,
until one day we rise to face it again.

Speaking the truth feels natural,
Unveils the evil we have been holding onto,
awaken to fall, unafraid to roll,
crossing the other side that is called,
Aligning with the art of coming home,
arriving just in time, to each her own.

Liberate

Sing when you are free, sing when you are caged,
sing when you are, just a little bit late,
because lessons are best learned from mistakes.

Don't wait for a person to be rich, famous or dead,
have your heart in the right place, that cares.

Love to not hold back,
love from wherever you are,
love that *Liberate* and sends you far.

Afterglow

Left behind to deal with where light disappears,
standing alone in the dark of my fears, as I let you go,
today.

Hope the glow sticks around on your face as we part
ways,
this feels right somehow even though it is tearing us
away.

As I hold the picture of the memories we made,
a smile shows up, shadowing the pain,
wishing you the very best, as I let you go, today.

Indifference

Extreme, we think as opposites,
love for hate, and care for hurt,
engaging in thought, that has it all.

Fall to the bottom, with a wake up call,
empty emotions, seeking *Indifference*.

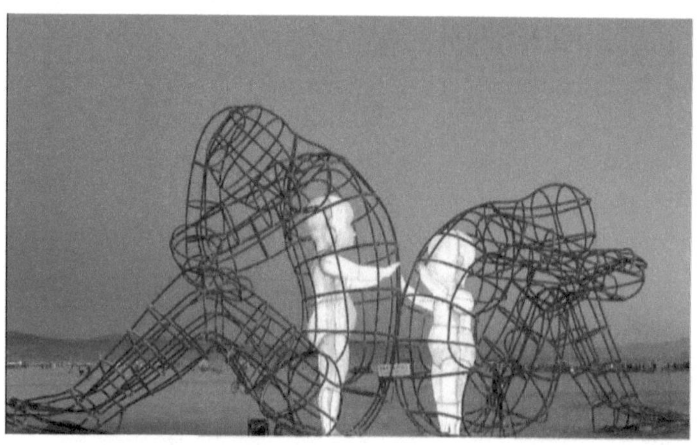

Conflict

Little one i was called,
bundle of joy was my reference,
unconditional love they presented,
and family was my existence.

Struggling to provide for a dream corner,
distanced themselves from one other,
I hear, my love kept them together,
yet, conveniently blamed me for being like the other.

Solace I gained in hobbies away from reality,
wish they stopped by to ask my difficulty,
holding on because of me, is not helping,
freedom I seek from this *Conflict*.

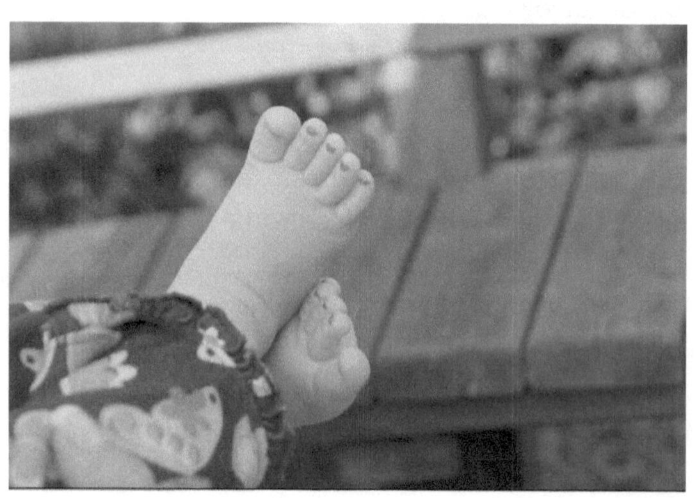

Journey

A girl with walls built around her,
rigid is the name she was known for,
black and white, seeing things crystal clear,
grey is the place, love pulled her over.

Breathing guilt day in and day out,
finding a balance to stand without,
lonely she found herself to be,
Love, she blamed for being the victim.

Love is fulfilling she just couldn't see,
walls she built and freedom she seeks?
she lost her balance time and again,
"Everything alright," she said to regain.

Healing is the journey she peregrinated over,
breaking the walls seems forever,
bringing herself home repeatedly,
finding herself strong, yet snivelling.

Love is indeed a *Journey* within.

Unfinished

Pulling away from reality,
we look for quite moments,
solace is felt in the pain,
memories hold us back in the game.

Even though we bite off more than we can chew,
we make a life big enough to live,
a pause is enough to stir up the lost emotions,
imagine an ending only to begin differently.

Dark nights brew incomplete stories,
connections unexplained and desires *Unfinished*.

Window

When the doors are closed, we look out for a breeze,
Open the window for fresh air from the trees,
accepting what cools us down for the time being,
for all we know, it might be a way out like a dream.

Imprint

Age humbles, leaving behind a scar,
Crow's feet show up when you laugh,
lessons we learn from being thrown,
rising again, standing alone,
Imprinting a story, to each, her own.

9 798889 777425 8